Warm &
sunny
to come

Goodnight Anna Maria Island

written and illustrated by

Phyllis Chandler Grey

Travel Writer and Photographer

ARTIST ROW
PUBLISHING

Goodnight
Anna Maria Island

Copyright 2015. 1st Revised Edition 2016. Phyllis Chandler Grey

All rights reserved. No part of this book may be reproduced in any form by any electronic or mechanical means including photocopying, recording, or information storage and retrieval without the prior written permission of the publisher.

PRINTED BY:
Anderson International Printing Group
3926 Valrico Grove Drive
Valrico, Florida 33594
glenn@andersoninternationalprinting.com

ISBN: 978-0-9909065-1

Designed on Anna Maria Island, Florida
United States of America

Printed in China

281.733.7800
phyllisgrey@gmail.com

Available through amazon.com/books

*Dedicated to the children who leave footprints
in the sand on Anna Maria Island
and especially to Gentry, Laudie, and Charlee Rose.
May you all have a lifetime of sweet island dreams.*

from the author of

Anna Maria Island
Sunrise to Sunset

Available through amazon.com/books

Goodnight
Anna Maria Island

written and illustrated by

Phyllis Chandler Grey

Travel Writer and Photographer

ARTIST ROW
PUBLISHING

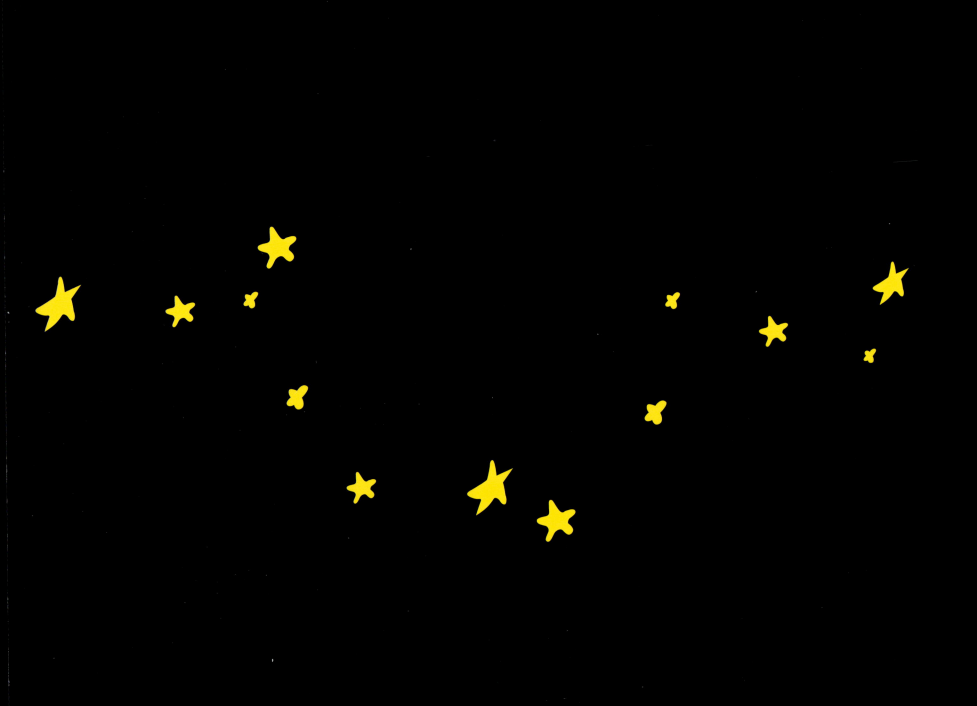

*L*ights out,
 the night's out.

We have had another
 great day.

So, dream now

and remember how

we played the time away.

Say 'goodnight'

to all we liked
 on Anna Maria Island.

Goodnight, Mr. Shark.
I saw you at the beach today.
You smiled at me,
then walked away.

Goodnight, Gulf of Mexico,

so clear,
 so aqua blue.

The waves roll in then
 sneak back out.

How we love to play in you!

Goodnight, shorebird.

You nest and feed on the beaches.

*Flying away at dusk,
    you'll return at dawn*

from dunes and keys and reaches.

Goodnight, shellers.
You walk the beach looking down
for treasures that have
    not been found.
You stoop and bend
    and load the sack,
and at the next low tide, you're back.

Goodnight, dunes and sea oats.
Dad says you shelter the birds
and hold the beach steady.

Mom agrees you do all that—
and make the shoreline pretty.

Goodnight, sea turtle.

You crawl to the shore
where you bury your eggs.

We find trails in the sand
from your strong flipper legs.

Goodnight, baby turtles,
   growing beneath the beach sand.

You struggle and climb from deep below,
   with your brothers and sisters pushing you so,

to the surface and to the light.

Goodnight, moon.

Your light is like a dome.

You guide the turtle hatchlings back to their sea home.

🌙 Goodnight, Mr. Ibis.
What a long curved bill!
You find crabs in the sand
and eat your fill.

Goodnight, bicycles.

The island is flat. We pedal with ease.

We enjoy our ride in the island breeze.

Goodnight, Mr. Dolphin, swimming up and swimming down,
circling like a merry-go-round.
The water is your big playground.

Goodnight, island artist.

You paint wonders like sunsets and gulls.

Mom hangs your paintings at home on our walls.

Goodnight, City Pier.

Visitors have enjoyed you for more than a hundred years.

Fishing, laughing and sharing tales, we dine and dance as the guitarist wails.

Goodnight, beach rental store,
filled with cool stuff for fun galore.

Goodnight, Surfer Bus, with paddle boards and kayaks just for us.

Goodnight, drawbridges, to name all three,
  Manatee, Cortez and Long Boat Key.

You raise to let the boats pass through,
  while cars wait behind the arms of you.

Goodnight, Free Trolley,
with riders so jolly,

running seven miles
from far to near,
from Coquina Beach
to the City Pier.

Goodnight, beach house,
  our home while on vacations.

We love to return each year,
  from many states and nations.

Goodnight, General Store. You have what we need and a whole lot more.

*Goodnight, sweet places,
   from island end to end,*

*with ice cream and candy,
   fudge and doughnuts,
   and sprinkles for my friend.*

Goodnight, blue heron, standing so tall.
 You are the best fisher of all.

With your knife-sharp bill
 and quick as a wink,

You spear your fish dinner
 before I can blink!

Goodnight, sunset.

Like magic, the sky turns orange, pink and blue,

While all watch with awe, the brilliance of you.

🌙 Goodnight, Miss Mermaid.

Don't know if I'm dreaming,
but I'll wear my goggles,

to see your eyes beaming.

🌙 Goodnight, Mr. Manatee,
   with tiny kind eyes.
You eat lots of veggies
   and swim the warm tides.

Goodnight, plumeria blossoms,
pink, yellow and white.
All over the island,
you're a welcoming sight.

Goodnight, festive beaches,
with wedding decorations.

Brides and grooms, family and friends,
gather for celebrations.

Goodnight, Mr. Pelican.

From high in the sky, you dive straight down.
  Just like a bomber, you are mission bound.

Hitting the water without an "ouch,"
  you pop to the top with a fish-filled pouch.

Goodnight, Rod and Reel Pier,

with fishing straight from heaven.

You are old and creaky like Grandma, also born in '47.

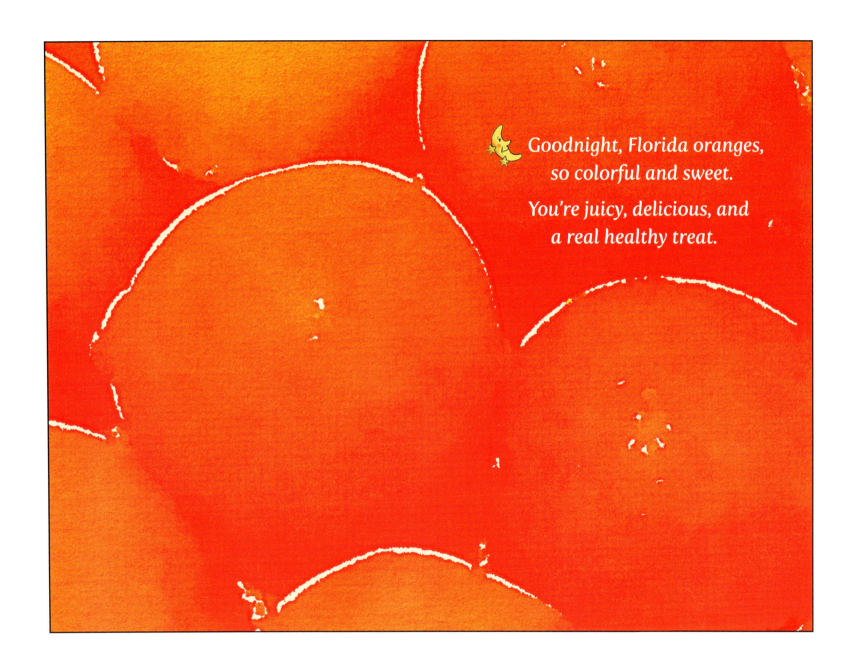

Goodnight, captains of fishing boats,
with fresh bait, rods and reels and floats.
We fish for grouper, snapper and snook.
You teach us how to set the hook.

Goodnight, little sprinting sanderling.
   Both feet leave the sand when you're running.

Smallest bird upon the shore,
   but fastest in the shorebird lore.

Goodnight, Marina.

Boat and yachts of every kind.
Wish that one of them was mine!

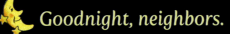 Goodnight, neighbors.

Goodnight, July Fourth Parade,
  with floats that are dandy.
Smiling pirates wave to us
  while throwing beads and candy.

*Goodnight, fireworks on the beaches.
  I hear "oohs" and "ahs" and screeches
from crowds that peer in the dark of night,
  watching bright sparkles taking flight.*

Goodnight, Anna Maria Island